First World War
and Army of Occupation
War Diary
France, Belgium and Germany

29 DIVISION
86 Infantry Brigade
Royal Warwickshire Regiment
53 Battalion
17 March 1919 - 1 October 1919

WO95/2302/5

The Naval & Military Press Ltd
www.nmarchive.com
Published in association with The National Archives

Published by

The Naval & Military Press Ltd

Unit 10 Ridgewood Industrial Park,

Uckfield, East Sussex,

TN22 5QE England

Tel: +44 (0) 1825 749494

www.naval-military-press.com

www.nmarchive.com

This diary has been reprinted in facsimile from the original. Any imperfections are inevitably reproduced and the quality may fall short of modern type and cartographic standards.

© Crown Copyright
Images reproduced by permission of The National Archives, London, England, 2015.

Contents

Document type	Place/Title	Date From	Date To
Heading	WO95/230/5		
Heading	Southern (Late 29th) Divn 86th Infy Bde 53rd Roy. Warwicks Mar-Sep 1919 From UK		
War Diary	Dover Dunkirk	17/03/1919	19/03/1919
War Diary	Mulheim	20/03/1919	20/03/1919
War Diary	Mulheim Berg Gladbach	21/03/1919	21/03/1919
War Diary	Berg Gladbach	22/03/1919	31/03/1919
Heading	War Diary. Month Of May 1919. Of 53rd. Royal Warwickshire Regiment.		
War Diary	Kurten	01/05/1919	17/05/1919
War Diary	B. Gladbach	18/05/1919	31/05/1919
War Diary	War Diary Month Of June 1919. Of 53rd. Battn. Royal Warwickshire Regiment.		
War Diary	Berg Gladbach	01/06/1919	10/06/1919
War Diary	Mulheim	11/06/1919	17/06/1919
War Diary	Berg Gladbach	18/06/1919	29/06/1919
Heading	War Diary. For Month Of July 1919. Of 53rd. Battn. Royal Warwickshire Regiment.		
War Diary	Mulheim Leverkusen & Dellbruck	01/07/1919	01/07/1919
War Diary	Mulheim	02/07/1919	17/07/1919
War Diary	Forward Area	18/07/1919	31/07/1919
Heading	War Diary. Month Of August 1919. 53rd. Battn. Royal Warwickshire Regiment.		
War Diary	Kurten	01/08/1919	15/08/1919
War Diary	Gladbach	16/08/1919	31/08/1919
War Diary	B. Gladbach	01/09/1919	13/09/1919
War Diary	Mulheim	14/09/1919	01/10/1919

W3095/2302/5

SOUTHERN (LATE 29TH) DIVN
86TH INFY BDE

53RD ROY. WARWICKS
MAR - SEP 1919

SOUTHERN DIVN.
53 R.Warwick Rgt
1/4
Mar - Sep 1919

WAR DIARY
INTELLIGENCE SUMMARY.
Army Form C. 2118.

(Erase heading not required.)

Instructions regarding War Diaries and Intelligence Summaries are contained in F.S. Regs., Part II. and the Staff Manual respectively. Title pages will be prepared in manuscript.

Place	Date	Hour	Summary of Events and Information	Remarks and references to Appendices
Dover / Dunkirk	17/3/19	14.00 / 16.50	Battalion embarked at Dover. Weather warm and bright. Landed at Dunkirk after a very smooth crossing. Proceeded to No 3A Rest Camp. The men were under canvas for the first time for the night.	
	18/3/19 19/3/19	13.45 hrs	Entrained at 13.45 hrs. Travelled via Cassel, Bailleul, Armentières, Lille, Mons, Namur, Liège, to Mulheim.	
Mulheim	20/3/19	06.30	Arrived at Mulheim. Battalion billeted in schools and houses.	Billetsgrund
Mulheim / Berg Gladbach	21/3/19	09.00 / 13.30 hrs	Battalion paraded by road to Berg Gladbach. Arrived in at 13.30 hrs. Billets good. Supplying guards at railhead and ration dump also a guard to stop all motors, as a result of a bank robbery but nothing was found.	Operation Order BO 2 SD 3
Berg Gladbach	22/3/19	—	Billeted at Berg Gladbach. Weather dull & cold. Battalion inspected by G.O.C. 14 Bde.	
Berg Gladbach	23/3/19	10.00	Billeted at Berg Gladbach. About two inches of snow in the morning. Battalion paraded for Divine Service. Weather bright snow soon cleared away.	
Berg Gladbach	24/3/19		Billeted at Berg Gladbach. Weather dull, some rain. Headquarter Company formed. Lewis gun, signalling & scout training started.	
Berg Gladbach	25/3/19		Billeted at Berg Gladbach. Weather dull. "A" Company inspected by Commanding Officer	

Army Form C. 2118.

WAR DIARY
or
INTELLIGENCE SUMMARY.

(Erase heading not required.)

Instructions regarding War Diaries and Intelligence Summaries are contained in F. S. Regs., Part II. and the Staff Manual respectively. Title pages will be prepared in manuscript.

Place	Date	Hour	Summary of Events and Information	Remarks and references to Appendices
Berg Gladbach	26/2/19		Billeted at Berg Gladbach. Weather wet & cold. Some snow during day. "B" Coy inspected by Commanding Officer.	
Berg Gladbach	27/2/19		Billeted at Berg Gladbach. Weather bright and warm in the morning but rain fell in the afternoon. "C" Company inspected by Commanding Officer.	
Berg Gladbach	28/2/19		Billeted at Berg Gladbach. Weather dull & cold. Some rain and sleet.	
Berg Gladbach	1/3/19		Billeted at Berg Gladbach. Weather dull & cold with some snow. Company Parades.	
Berg Gladbach	2/3/19	0930	Billeted at Berg Gladbach. About six inches of snow fell during night. Church Parade.	
Berg Gladbach	3/3/19		Billeted at Berg Gladbach. Weather dull, some snow fell during day. Company training.	

2/4/19
Berg Gladbach

Williams Lieut Colonel
Commanding 23rd Royal Warwickshire Regiment

Cover for Documents.

Nature of Enclosures.

WAR DIARY.

Month of May 1919.

of

53rd. Royal Warwickshire Regiment.

Notes, or Letters written.

Army Form C. 2118.

WAR DIARY
or
INTELLIGENCE SUMMARY.
(Erase heading not required)

Instructions regarding War Diaries and Intelligence Summaries are contained in F. S. Regs., Part II. and the Staff Manual respectively. Title pages will be prepared in manuscript.

Place	1919	Hour	Summary of Events and Information	Remarks and references to Appendices
Kurten	MAY 1		Battalion billeted in Kurten. Company training. Weather dull	
do.	2		- do - -do- Weather dull	
do.	3		- do - -do- Weather fine	
do.	4		- do - -do-	
do.	5		- do - -do- Weather fine	
do.	6		- do - -do- Weather warm	
do.	7		- do - -do-	
do.	8		- do - -do- Weather hot.	
do.	9		- do - -do- Weather hot.	
do.	10		- do - -do- Weather hot.	
do.	11		- do - Weather hot.	
do.	12		- do - -do- Weather hot.	
do.	13		Battalion relieved in Kurten area moved to billets in Gladbach (Paper Factory). Weather hot. Relief complete by 21-30 hours.	J.F.
do.	14		Battalion billeted in Berg Gladbach (Paper Factory) Company training and baths for battalion	J.F.
do.	15		- do - -do- Transport inspected by	J.F.
			the Commanding Officer of No. 2 Company Train.	J.F.
do.	16		Battalion billeted in Gladbach, Weather hot Company training.	J.F.
do.	17		- do - -do-	J.F.

Army Form C. 2118.

WAR DIARY
or
INTELLIGENCE SUMMARY.
(Erase heading not required.)

Instructions regarding War Diaries and Intelligence Summaries are contained in F. S. Regs., Part II. and the Staff Manual respectively. Title pages will be prepared in manuscript.

Place	Date 1919 May	Hour	Summary of Events and Information	Remarks and references to Appendices
B.GLADBACH	18		Battalion billeted in Berg Gladbach . Weather warm .Church parade in Mariensaal.	
do.	19		Battalion billeted in Berg Gladbach . Weather warm .Company training	
do.	20		Battalion billeted in Berg Gladbach . Weather still very warm. Company training.	
do.	21		Battalion billeted in Berg Gladbach . C in C.'s inspection cancelled .The C.O. inspected the battalion at 09-15 hours on R.F.A.football ground. Company training rest of day.	
do.	22		Battalion billeted in Berg Gladbach . Weather very hot . Company training	
do.	23		Battalion billeted in Berg Gladbach . Weather hot. Company training	
do.	24		Battalion billeted at Berg Gladbach .Weather hot .C.in C,'s inspection.Company training as usual	
do.	25		Battalion Billeted at Berg Gladbach. Church parade in Mariensaal.	
do.	26		Battalion billeted at Berg Gladbach.,100 Other Ranks trip up Rhine starting from Bonn. Weather hot. Company training.	
do.	27		Battalion billeted at Berg Gladbach.Weather hot.Company training.	
do.	28		Battalion billeted at Berg Gladbach.Weather hot. Company training.	
do.	29		Battalion Billeted at Berg Gladbach.Weather hot. Company training.	
do.	30		Battalion Billeted at Berg Gladbach Weather hot. Company training.	
do.	31		Battalion billeted at Berg Gladbach Weather hot .Company training	

1/6/19

Charles Higgins
Lieut.Colonel.
Commanding 53rd.Battalion The Royal Warwickshire Regiment.

Cover for Documents.

Nature of Enclosures.

WAR DIARY.

MONTH OF JUNE 1919.
OF

53rd. Battn. ROYAL WARWICKSHIRE REGIMENT.

Army Form W.3091.

Notes, or Letters written.

53rd R Warwickshire Regt.

Army Form C. 2118.

WAR DIARY
or
INTELLIGENCE SUMMARY.
(Erase heading not required.)

Instructions regarding War Diaries and Intelligence Summaries are contained in F. S. Regs., Part II. and the Staff Manual respectively. Title pages will be prepared in manuscript.

Place	Date	Hour	Summary of Events and Information	Remarks and references to Appendices
Bury Gladbach	Jan 1st		Church parade	
"	2nd		"A" & "B" Coys went to Exercise Platz Mülheim under Maj Warr, M.C. for work on Div" Rath Course. Coys under Canvass	C.H. C.H.
"	3		"B" Coy training. "D" coy Squad drills	
"	4			
"	5		Capt. Edsell Hanks RA reported for duty as adjutant	C.H
"	6		Major Dodin DSO relinquished appt of 2 i.c. command Surrender to England. Divisional Race	C.H
"	7		Divisional Race — fine thro' week	
"	8		Church Parade	C.H
"	9		"C" & "D" coys moved to Leverkusen and Dellbrück respectively in Relief of 1 company of 51st Royal Warwick	C.H
"	10		HQ "A" & "B" coys marched to Mülheim and completed relief of 51st R. Warwick	C.H

Army Form C. 2118.

WAR DIARY
or
INTELLIGENCE SUMMARY.

(Erase heading not required.)

Instructions regarding War Diaries and Intelligence Summaries are contained in F.S. Regs., Part II. and the Staff Manual respectively. Title pages will be prepared in manuscript.

Place	Date	Hour	Summary of Events and Information	Remarks and references to Appendices
Malheim	Jan 11"		All coy finding guard duties - 1 night in bed	
"	12		Inspection of T.O. by C.O.	
"	13		Guard duties	
"	14		do	
"	15		do	
"	16		do	
"	17		Adv. guard relieved by 1st Bn. K.R.R.C. in preparation for move forward	
Ing Gladbach	18		Batt. marched to Burg Gladbach on relief, and went into scattered billets. v. hot day	
"	19		Bn. moved billets to Maria Saal & School area - found much	
"	20		for following day cancelled. Adv. corps training. Major Watts returned from leave.	
"	21		Church parade. Coy training. Musketry	
"	22		Church parade.	

Army Form C. 2118.

WAR DIARY
or
INTELLIGENCE SUMMARY.
(Erase heading not required)

Instructions regarding War Diaries and Intelligence Summaries are contained in F. S. Regs., Part II. and the Staff Manual respectively. Title pages will be prepared in manuscript.

Place	Date	Hour	Summary of Events and Information	Remarks and references to Appendices
Burg Hulshout	23		Coy training. Divies Mountains	
"	24		do	
"	25		do	
"	26		Batn. Route march (11 amile)	
"	27		Hol day. Corp $ + T training. Bric inspection	
"	28		Peace S'Gaude	
"	29		Church Parade	

Clark Moore Lt Col

(6414) Wt. W3906/P1607 2,500,000 7/18 McA & W Ltd (E 3591) Forms W3091/4.   Army Form W.3091.

Cover for Documents.

Nature of Enclosures.

WAR DIARY.

FOR

MONTH OF JULY 1919.

OF

53rd. Battn. ROYAL WARWICKSHIRE REGIMENT.

Notes, or Letters written.

Army Form C. 2118.

WAR DIARY
or
INTELLIGENCE SUMMARY.
(Erase heading not required.)

Instructions regarding War Diaries and Intelligence Summaries are contained in F. S. Regs., Part II. and the Staff Manual respectively. Title pages will be prepared in manuscript.

Place	Date	Hour	Summary of Events and Information	Remarks and references to Appendices
MULHEIM	JULY 1st		Battn: settles down in new billets. "A" & "B" Coys relieve each other in guard duties in the Mulheim area.	
LEVERKUSEN & DELLBRUCK			"C" & "D" Coys find guards in the Leverkusen and Dellbruck areas, respectively.	
MULHEIM	2nd		Training carried out as far as possible. Lt: Col: U.G.Higgins.C.M.G.,D.S.O. goes on leave; Major R.G. Watts. M.C. takes over command of the Battalion.	
"	3rd		Guard duties and Company Training.	
"	4th:		Guard duties and Company Training.	
"	5th		Company Training for men not on guard.	
"	6th		Church Parade for Companies in MULHEIM.	
"	7th		Rhine Trip for seven or eight officers and 100 men.	
"	8th		Peace Holiday for men not on guard.	
"	9th		Peace Holiday for men not on guard.	
"	10th		Company training and Guards.	
"	11th		Company training and Guards.	
"	12th		Company training and Guards.	
"	13th		Church Parade.	
"	14th		Education Examinations for 2nd: and 3rd: Class Certificates.	
"	15th		Education Examinations for 2nd and 3rd: Class Certificates.	
"	16th		"D" Company moves to LEVERKUSEN. All guards relieved in Mulheim area by 52 R.W.R	

Army Form C. 2118.

WAR DIARY
or
INTELLIGENCE SUMMARY.
(Erase heading not required.)

Instructions regarding War Diaries and Intelligence
Summaries are contained in F. S. Regs., Part II.
and the Staff Manual respectively. Title pages
will be prepared in manuscript.

Place	Date	Hour	Summary of Events and Information	Remarks and references to Appendices
MULHEIM	JULY 17th		Battalion moves to forward area. "HQ" to Kurten, "A" Coy to Bechen, "B" Coy to Junkermuhle, "C" Company to Wipperfeld and "D" Company to Forsten.	
FORWARD AREA	18th		Training commenced.	
"	19th		Peace Day. General Holiday granted.	
"	20th		Church Services for all Companies.	
"	21st		Training, somewhat hampered by the weather.	
"	22nd		Training, somewhat hampered by the weather.	
"	23rd		Training, somewhat hampered by the weather. Lt: Col: C.G.Higgins.C.M.G.,D.S.O. returned from leave and assumed Command of the Battalion.	
"	24th		Commanding Officer visited "A", "B", "C" and "D" Companies.	
"	25th		Commanding Officer visited "A" Company at Bechen.	
"	26th		Battalion Sports.	
"	27th		Sunday. Very wet day. Church services for all Companies.	
"	28th		Coy. Training. Major R.O.Watts.M.C. proceeded on leave. Commenced training for Div: Sports.	
"	29th		Coy. Training. Draft of 20 O.R. arrived from 1st Bn: R.War.R. from ENGLAND.	
"	30th		Company Training.	
"	31st		Company Training.	

Charl. Higgins
Lieut: Colonel.
Commanding 53rd: Battalion The Royal Warwickshire Regiment.

(6414) Wt. W3906/P1607 2,500,000 7/18 McA & W Ltd (E 3591) Forms W3091/4.   Army Form W.3091.

Cover for Documents.

Nature of Enclosures.

WAR DIARY.

MONTH OF AUGUST 1919.

53rd. Battn. ROYAL WARWICKSHIRE REGIMENT.

Notes, or Letters written.

Army Form C. 2118.

WAR DIARY
or
INTELLIGENCE SUMMARY.
(Erase heading not required).

Instructions regarding War Diaries and Intelligence Summaries are contained in F. S. Regs. Part II. and the Staff Manual respectively. Title pages will be prepared in manuscript.

Place	Date	Hour	Summary of Events and Information	Remarks and references to Appendices
KURTEN	1/8/19		Fine day. Lewis Gun class started.	
	2/8/19		Wet day.	
	3/8/19		Sunday. All Companies Divine service.	
	4/8/19		Bank Holiday.	
	5/8/19		Company Training.	
	6/8/19		All day and night scheme for Battalion Signallers	
	7/8/19		Company Training	
	8/8/19		Divisional Tournament	
	9/8/19		"	
	10/8/19		Sunday. Divine Service for all Companies.	
	11/8/19		Company Training.	
	12/8/19		Company Training. Examination of Examination Class.	
	13/8/19		Company Training.	
	14/8/19		"	
Gladbach	15/8/19		Battalion relieved by the 52nd.Bn.R.War.R. and marched to Berg Gladbach on relief	
	16/8/19		Interior Economy. Selection of Guard of Honour for Army Council.	
	17/8/19		Sunday. Divine Service.	
	18/8/19		Brig.Gen.Campbell inspected the Guard of Honour for Army Council, very hot.	
	19/8/19		Army Council visited Battalion inspected men at teas. Battalion provided a Guard of Honour of 3 Officers, and 100 Other Ranks at Divisional H.Q. Commander Capt.Settle. Very hot day.	
	20/8/19		Commanding Officers parade. 09-00hours. Remainder of day holiday.	
	21/8/19		Commanding Officer leaves Battalion to take Command of 1stSouthern Infantry Brigade during absence of Brig.Gen.Campbell on leave.	
	22/8/19		Beds are fitted up in the Barrack Rooms.	
	23/8/19		Company Training	
	24/8/19		Inspection of Barracks. Cricket match v 52nd.Bn.R.War.R. (lost)	
	25/8/19		Sunday Wet day Divine Service.	
	29/8/19		Training and Guards.	
	30/8/19		"D" Company proceed to DELLBRUCK for Musketry.	
	31/8/19		Sunday. Divine Service	

Watts Major.
Commanding 53rd. Battalion The Royal Warwickshire Regiment.

Army Form C. 2118.

WAR DIARY
~~INTELLIGENCE SUMMARY~~
(Erase heading not required.)

Instructions regarding War Diaries and Intelligence Summaries are contained in F.S. Regs., Part II. and the Staff Manual respectively. Title pages will be prepared in manuscript.

5³ R. Warwick

Place	Date	Hour	Summary of Events and Information	Remarks and references to Appendices
B.Gladbach	1/9/19		78 O.R.proceed on leave	
"	2/9/19		71 O.R.proceed on leave	
"	3/9/19		Guard duties leave very few for training which is carried out by what men there are in the Bn.	
"	4/9/19			
"	5/9/19		Colonel C.G.Higgins returns from Brigade and assumes command of Battalion	
"	6/9/19		Guards – very hot week.	
"	7/9/19		Divine service "C" Company move to DELLBRUCK to fire G.M.C. "D" Coy. returned to GLADBACH.	
"	8/9/19			
"	9/9/19		80 O.R.proceed on leave.	
"	10/9/19			
"	11/9/19			
12/9/19			"C"Coy on ~~xxxxx~~ conclusion of musketry move to FLITTARD in relief of 1 Coy. of 51.st R.War.R. Guard at Gladbach relieved by 52nd.R.War.R. 27 O.R. go on leave.	
"	13/9/19		Battalion relieved by 52nd R.War.R.and on relief moved to Infantry Barracks MULHEIM ."C"Coy at Flittard – very hot week 257 B.R. on leave	
MULHEIM	14/9/19		Divine Service	
"	15/9/19		Guard duties.	
"	16/9/19		Lt.Col.Higgins proceeds to BRUSSELLS for 4 or 5 days .A case of diptheria suspected and 14 men isolated.	
"	17/9/19		Guard duties	
"	18/9/19		do. do. do.	
"	19/9/19		"D" Coy.relieves "C" Coy. at FLITTARD ."C" Coy.returns to MULHEIM ."C" Coy.returns to MULHEIM and undertakes guard duties here.Men begin to arrive back from leave "A" Coy.goes to the DELLBRUCK Musketry Range.	
"	20/9/19			
"	21/9/19		Sunday Very few men available for Divine service .Very wet and cold in the evening ."A" Coy do some good shooting at the Range.	
"	22/9/19		Guard duties .Some more men return from leave.	
"	23/9/19		do.	
"	24/9/19		"A" Company on the range commence Part lll	
"	25/9/19		Guard duties and training.	
"	26/9/19		do.	

(continued)

Army Form C. 2118.

WAR DIARY
or
INTELLIGENCE SUMMARY.
(Erase heading not required.)

Instructions regarding War Diaries and Intelligence Summaries are contained in F. S. Regs., Part II. and the Staff Manual respectively. Title pages will be prepared in manuscript.

Place	Date	Hour	Summary of Events and Information	Remarks and references to Appendices
MULHEIM	27/9/19		"B" Coy. moves to DELLBRUCK for musketry :"A" Coy. takes over the Guards at Flittard :"D"Coy return to MULHEIM BARRACKS	a.S.
"	28/9/19		Sunday .Very wet no men available for church parade.	a.S.
"	29/9/19		A platoon of "B" Coy.(No 8) return from DELLBRUCK for preparation for the Tournout and Drill Competition.	a.S.
"	30/9/19		The Transport is inspected for the Transport Competition Rhine Army Championship.	a.S.

MULHEIM
1/10/19

[signature] Lieut.Colonel,
Commanding 53rd. Battalion The Royal Warwickshire Regiment.

www.ingramcontent.com/pod-product-compliance
Lightning Source LLC
Chambersburg PA
CBHW081252170426
43191CB00037B/2130